Ballad of a Bighorn Guide: Poems with Fins

Ballad of a Bighorn Guide: Poems with Fins

Harry Piper

Copyright © 2009 by Harry Piper.

Text and preface, copyright © 2009 by Harry Piper.

Foreword, copyright © 2009 by Barry & Cathy Beck.

Library of Congress Control Number: 2009906059
ISBN: Softcover   978-1-4415-3856-7

Cover color image and interior black and white images "Buckingham's Copper John" giclee print (18 X 24 inches) by A.D. Maddox, www.admaddox.com.

First printing. All rights reserved. No part of this book may be reproduced without written permission of the author, except excerpts as needed for reviews.

Thanks to the editors of the following publications in which some of these poems have appeared or been accepted for publication: *Jefferson Monthly* ("First Coast Steelhead," "To a Dead King Salmon"), *Gray's Sporting Journal* ("Battle on Florida Bay").

Copies of this book can be obtained from the Author for the cost of shipping only, for use in raffles or in exchange for donations, by Whirling Disease Foundation (WDF), Trout Unlimited or any of its chapters, Casting for Recovery (CFR) or any of its retreat groups, Warriors and Quiet Waters Foundation, Project Healing Waters, Bighorn River Alliance, or any other fly fishing-related organization deemed worthy by the Author, with all proceeds going to such organization or local chapter. Author's portion of sales through bookstores and internet outlets such as Amazon.com will be split between WDF and CFR. Contact the Author at 1399 Hwy 234, Eagle Point, OR 97524, (541) 830-1993, fax 826-2205, *shaggysntrout@aol.com*.

This book was printed in the United States of America.

To order additional copies of this book, contact:
Xlibris Corporation
1-888-795-4274
www.Xlibris.com
Orders@Xlibris.com
62160

Contents

Preface 13
Foreword 15
Casting for Recovery 17
Whirling Disease 19

First Casts

Five Meditations on Water 23
Sonnet to Tiktaalik 25
The Sense of It 26
Lake Lydiard, 1958 27
Driftless Daydreams 28
Y Montana? 29
Charlie Fetch 30

Trout

The Trout 33
Dillon 1963 34
Spawning Rainbows 36
Kinni Trip 37
Evening Hatch on the Willow 38
A Kinnickinnic Life 39
The Encounter 40
Bighorn 1, You 0 42
Below the Bighorn Afterbay 43
Ballad of a Bighorn Guide 44
To the Bighorn Cabin, Burned 46

Steelhead and Salmon

Tying a Steelhead Fly 49
King of the Pier in Manitowoc 50

Clearwater Reverie 51
To a Wild Hen Steelhead 52
The Big One That 53
First Coast Steelhead 54
Salmon Love 55
To a Dead King Salmon 56

The Salt

Battle on Florida Bay, 1976 59
Magnificent Frigate-Bird 60
In Mexico After Too Much Rum I Obsess About
    Tomorrow's Fishing 61
GT Quickstep 62
The Answer 63

Last Casts

Fish Mystics 67
Yellowstone Pictures 68
A Lone Fisherman Not Alone 69
Lake Michigan Vespers 71
The Eagle 72
Do Not Go Gentle 73

About the Author 75

For Mike Pflaum (1944-2009), my oldest fishing buddy,
Datus Proper (1934-2003), friend and author of classics,
and Gael Larr (1953-2002), the best guide ever.

If I hold the book up like this, can you guys see all right?

And for my Mary and all other breast cancer survivors
who fly fish or would like to.

More Praise for *Ballad of a Bighorn Guide: Poems with Fins:*

"It took me back to my youth, fishing with my father at sea, and fishing little Irish streams. I admit to some tears too—good memories. This book would have been fun to share with Datus; he would have enjoyed it tremendously, as I did."
　　　　　　　　　　　　　　　　Anna Collins-Proper, Bozeman, Montana

"Really brought back some personal memories. Nice work for a great cause."
　　　　　　　　　　　　Bob Quigley, fly tier and author, Ashland, Oregon

"A book that anglers will enjoy. The ones that really touched me were Ballad of a Bighorn Guide, Sonnet to Tiktaalik, Spawning Rainbows, The Ballad of Big Lewis, To the Bighorn Cabin, Burned, Clearwater Reverie, To A Dead King Salmon, The Answer, A Lone Fisherman Not Alone, and Do Not Go Gentle."
　　　　　　Tom Morgan, rodsmith, former owner of R.L. Winston Rod Co., Bozeman, Montana

"I find the little stories very refreshing. The writing and subject matter [bring] the reader along . . . on this poetic journey of fishing and life. Nicely done!"
　　　　　　　　Bob Jacklin, Jacklin's Outfitters, West Yellowstone, Montana

"I read each page like a hungry brook trout drunk on Mayflies after ice out. I've lived these words, but it takes me 30 minutes in my TV show to accomplish, somewhat, what Harry Piper does in a page or two. His words made me happy, sad, excited, curious, worried, satisfied, victorious, playful, young, old, reflective, mischievous, and more. I even learned a thing or two. (I googled Tiktaalik as well as a few other things.) This book tells the secrets of an angler's heart and gives voice to what all fishermen know but can't say. For the lucky ones of us who spend quiet time in the great out of doors, we have Harry Piper's words to help explain [it] to the rest of the world—the noteworthy and at times humorous observations of a great sportsman."

    Kathryn Maroun, producer and president of What A Catch TV, Toronto, Ontario

"The poems . . . chart the seasons and phases of an angler's life with wit and reverence for the special places and people within them. This book is a wonderful collection of poetic insights, grounded in the daily and seasonal rituals known best to serious anglers."

    Charles Gauvin, president, Trout Unlimited, Arlington, Virginia

"It is so apparent that Harry Piper's words were inspired by the heart, flowed through the pen, then on to the pages of this beautiful work. Reading them, past moments of my life in the great outdoors were once again brought back to life."

    Frank Moore, fisherman and conservationist, Idlewyld Park, Oregon

"I was reminded of so many fishing experiences of the past. It also painted in words so many images burned in my memory. This work will reawaken our dreams of all those wonderful days we have spent on our rivers and streams."

    John Bailey, owner, Dan Bailey's Fly Shop, Livingston, Montana

"Rivers and the inhabitants of the watery elements are made for wise men to contemplate and for fools to pass by without consideration."
—Izaak Walton, *The Compleat Angler*

"I fish because I love to . . . not because I regard fishing as being so terribly important but because I suspect that so many of the other concerns of men are equally unimportant—and not nearly so much fun."
—Robert Traver, *Trout Madness*

"The charm of fishing is that it is the pursuit of what is elusive but attainable, a perpetual series of occasions for hope."
—Sir John Buchan, Lord Tweedsmuir

Preface

Poetry should fit the short attention span of modern readers. It's really just a condensed and heightened form of storytelling. I hope you like my mini fish stories. Thank you for "buying" my book by making your donation (suggested amount at least $20) to the Whirling Disease Foundation (WDF), which makes grants to support scientific research into this disease that attacks the coldwater fish we love, to Casting for Recovery (CFR), which puts on free fly fishing retreats for breast cancer survivors, or to some other worthy fishing-related organization. If you bought it at a bookstore or online, know that the Author's portion of the sale proceeds will be split between WDF and CFR.

Many of these poems, or earlier versions of them, were written a long time ago. My wife Mary's recent bout with breast cancer on top of my own earlier bout with prostate cancer convinced me not to wait any longer to collect them, along with newer ones, into a book. Thanks to Mary, my first and most important reader, and to those quoted in "advance praise" for looking over the manuscript and sending me their comments.

My friend Dave Wang, an excellent spey caster and fisherman, recently caught the biggest steelhead of his life, a wild male of 39 7/8 inches with a girth over 20 inches, certainly over 20 pounds, in the North Umpqua's flies-only water. (Hey, it was probably almost as big as the fish I hooked on the Clearwater. See "The Big One That . . . .") Catching a fish like that in nearby public waters on the swing, with his own hand-tied fly, is a great accomplishment. But I like it even more as a sign of health in the Umpqua system. Last winter Dave and I drove four hours up to the Portland area to testify in favor of a no-kill regulation for wild steelhead on the Umpqua. We and the others who testified (including Peter Tronquet of the Steamboaters club, Bill Bakke of the Native Fish Society, and guide Scott Howell) were successful; the no-kill regulation is now in place for at least four more years. British Columbia in its wisdom already has such a regulation.

Dams blocking fish passage to spawning grounds are being removed from rivers like the Penobscot in Maine and the Rogue, my home river in Oregon. The battle is on to save salmon and steelhead runs up the Columbia which supply fish to some of our most exciting rivers including the Deschutes, the John Day, the Snake, the Salmon, the Grande Ronde, and the Clearwater. The world angling community is more aware than ever of how fragile our great fisheries are, and yet how robust they can become when the right measures are taken.

Our souls expand with the pursuit of fish in their wild places. My stingy lawyer's heart began to dance when I drove up to Pennsylvania's Falling Springs Creek from Washington, D.C., or when I crossed into Wisconsin from the Twin Cities to stand in the Kinnickinnic, the Willow, or the Rush. If it weren't for fishing I wouldn't have met personal heroes like Tom Morgan and Frank Moore. I hope my poems convey that people and places like these are not just memories. They are as much a part of me as my blood.

If we are good enough stewards, our grandchildren's children will one day tremble with anticipation as they thread a fly line through the guides.

HCP, Eagle Point, Oregon, March 2009

Foreword

I must admit that when I sat down last night to look this book over, I told myself I could do this in ten minutes as it was being squeezed in during the three days at home between two long trips which I was not ready for at all.

I sat down at my desk and, as I usually do, started at the back and worked forward. When I came to the Ballad of a Bighorn Guide, I got choked up. I found Barry in the office editing images and tried to read it out loud to him and had to stop a couple of times. We didn't know Gael well, but we saw him often on the river and he always had a pleasant two-minute conversation with us. After the Ballad poem I told Barry "You have to hear this one too" and read Lake Michigan Vespers, and so it went with me reading and him listening.

Harry Piper has taken the curses and the blessings of fly fishing and turned them into beautiful poetry. Whether it's a snarl in one's leader or the quiet calm of a predawn boat ride to a favorite fishing spot, everyone will be reminded of a memory of their own in his writing.

Barry & Cathy Beck
Benton, Pennsylvania
March, 2009

casting for recovery

for mary, karyn k, and jean l.

you find a little lump
on your breast and have it
checked out
it turns out to be
cancer
they do an mri and find
more lumps on both sides
next thing you know
your husband is waving at you
as you're wheeled in
you wake up and feel your chest
they're gone
everyone is so kind
they bring you food
then you start chemo
you're not hungry any more
you look in the mirror
there's so much bruising
everything's misshapen and your hair
falls out in the shower and you get
tired
everyone says they understand
but they don't
except maybe the dogs
you can't keep up

your family gets cranky after a while
it's been a long time
they look at you
as if there might be something
wrong
a friend invites you to casting for recovery
it seems like an effort
but you go
when you're tired you rest
you even have fun it's something new
you're not very good but
it doesn't matter
you don't feel like people are
looking at you
on the last day a small trout actually
takes your fly
its jerky pull surprises you
it doesn't give up
you cradle it underwater
it's cool and slippery
and pretty
you ease the hook out
to let her go
and say a little prayer

Whirling Disease

for Dave K, Dick V, Barry N, Ron H, Mansoor,
Jerri B, and all soldiers in the WD wars

We used to think whirling disease
was only in the hatcheries. Wrong.
It showed up in the Madison
in the early 90's and was already
all over in Colorado. It hit
wild trout like smallpox hit the Indians.
A group of dedicated anglers started
the Whirling Disease Foundation in 1995.
The first symposium in Bozeman
got everybody talking and raised
money for research. We found out
nature is as elegant in killing
as she is in birth and life. The spores
of WD, strong as hockey pucks,
are eaten by aquatic worms
whose insides turn the pucks
to sets of little hooks called TAMs
tuned by temperature and nature's clock
to be released when trout are most
vulnerable on the spawning beds
so new fry are infected en masse.
Mansoor El-Matbouli in Germany
working under a WDF grant
found rainbows in a hatchery who had
built up resistance. These are being crossed
like all our fingers with wild rainbows
in the Gunnison. So far they're passing on
resistance from one generation
to another. We still need solutions
for Cutthroats and the Whitefish, so let's
keep the research going!

First Casts

Five Meditations on Water

1. In Genesis, water
covered the void before the Spirit
hovered over it
to speak the Word.

        2. When I recite the Nicene Creed
        "through him all things were made"
        I think of Thompson Creek with gratitude.

3. Water is 80 percent of us
Water's cycle is continuous
Thus 80 percent of us
is Metolius.

        4. An old sailor said he saw
        a flaming rainbow
        whose arch did reach
        to the bottom of the Mariana Trench.

5. If not for H_2O
all the animal orders
from earth's four corners
and all plants that grow
away would blow.

Sonnet to Tiktaalik

I always knew that I was part fish.
Tiktaalik Roseae, the fish with flippers
fossilized up in the Canadian Arctic,
confirms it. Human arms, wrists, and hands
evolved from these flippers. Human teeth
grew from spiky structures in the mouths
of lamprey-like creatures: conodonts.
Our larynx is composed of cartilege
akin to the gills in fish or shark.
If it weren't for great grandfather fish,
I couldn't talk or hold this very pen
or set the hook and reel a fish in
or bang away at typewriter keys.
Reason enough for catch and release.

The Sense of It

When summer is over
and winter's spate has taken over,
dark water covers the hole
that usually holds
a fish reached with a long cast
over that big rock and past
the heavy current into the slower water
against the far bank. The mother
of all fish might be there
right now you never know.
I'm standing in the water now
ready to throw
imaginary casts to that
sweet spot
glowing in my mind
with a fish still bright from the sea, the kind
that makes a year
or even a fishing life. You're
with me as I point
to the place. You don't
really have to be there, isn't it almost
better to lift your arm and toast
the perfect cast after you mentally make it
all the way across to the fish and never break it
off in the first run
and the long fight before you slide it in
to the shallows at your feet
where these lines record your feat?

Lake Lydiard, 1958

Slow windows candle us down the stairs
to gulp juice and donuts, gather our rods
and metal frog box. In the window well's
wet smell me and Mike trap frogs.
Then our flashlight plays across
the lawn, the dark trunks of oaks,
the electric fence we have to crawl
under. There's the garter snake:
Hey Ralph, how's the wife and kids?
By now our shoes and pants are wet with dew.
We circle poison ivy, duck the sumac
and there she is, the old wooden rowboat
smooth with all our sanding.
We slide her through the cattails and stop
to watch a big raccoon wash a bass.
We didn't build the dock high enough,
so our feet are wet when we get into the boat.
The air—humid, bullfrog-loud—muffles
the long trilling call of a redwing blackbird.
Two snapping turtles are grappling,
one on top of the other, jaws open.
We know what they're doing and laugh.
Bats veer home. Abandoned goose nests
top the beaver houses. Big mouths
bump the lily pads, hunting frogs
like ours cast out
in their little harnesses.

Driftless Daydreams

My mind is always moving out of houses,
away from battlements, silences
and verbal executions, to memories
of dappled baby crappies fat as hands,
sunnies nibbling nipples under the dock,
slippery brown bullheads' weird whiskers,
and largemouth bass dressed in mossy green
with a blurred black line along the seam.

Sometimes I go back to Walleyed Pike.
I knew an ice fisherman who spent
a long night on Lake Mille Lacs. The ice
cracked around his truck and fish house
till he was floating on an ice island.
He broke apart that house stick by stick
to keep a fire going and caught his limit.
Those walleyes tasted real good, you bet.

Or picture Northern Pike, the toothy jack
with mean black eyes in a flat head.
Half the fight of small ones we call snakes
is banging in the boat, scattering tackle.
Bigger ones patrol the lily pads
or watch for hours from cabbage weed
to snatch a baby duck or your Lazy Ike.
I close my eyes to see the quick strike.

Y Montana?

The lures of Montana—the Marlboro Man,
the movie A River Runs Through It,
wide open spaces and leathery faces,
Charlie Russell and others who drew it,
the wild mustang horses, the cavalry forces'
big battle at Custer's last stand,
wild Indians to fight, the Big Sky at night,
and owning your own piece of land—
all these conspire to create a desire
in the breast of the Dude of the East.
He can't wait to move, if only to prove
the cowboy within is a beast.

Charlie Fetch

Charlie Dog and I are driving
back from the Bighorn River
where we used to hunt ducks.
Now we mostly watch them through the window
or through the tall grass by the river.
Charlie cocks his head and whines
when ducks fly by. We both know
he can't swim far enough any more
to retrieve them, except in Lab dreams.
(He yips and jerks his legs by the fire.)

Twenty miles from home
we're not yet ready for family clamor
so I take the Livingston exit
and walk Charlie through the yellow grass.
He looks at me as if we share
a mental tennis ball: throw it far,
then fetch it back many years later.
Good boy Charlie!

Trout

The Trout

Nature's perfect creature is the trout.
These sleek not-water spaces in the creek
hold in the eternal now
or crossed by currents turn the other cheek.

Weightless they can flash from deep
to shallow and back, from black to blue
to black. Through turbulent and steep
these hydrobatic arrows fly true.

Their slipstream subtleties are home-grown:
Cutthroats' cuts on pepper-speckled yellows,
Browns buttered all the way down,
Brookies' red dots in purple halos,

and Rainbows' red sash across their silver.
Splashy stripes and spots of many kinds
show the Master's brushes color
outside the lines.

Dillon 1963

After summer jobs in Minneapolis
Mike and I drove to Dillon, Montana
in search of trout. At The Mint (well, maybe
it wasn't The Mint, but every Montana town
has one) we saw the friendly bartender
lend ten bucks on the spot
to a young woman down on her luck.
We asked about the fishing. He reached beneath
the bar for a box of flies he said would work.
We steamed them in our room at the Metlen,
the old hotel originally built to house
railroad employees, with a false front
and the longest bar in these United States.
The clerk at the front desk had metal teeth
that out-gleamed his eyes when he smiled.
We walked along the tracks outside of town,
hot as hell in our baggy rubber waders,
and slid the steep bank to the Beaverhead.
It looked to us like a river in Wisconsin—
smooth and deep, a clay and gravel bottom,
and weeping willows hanging all the way
down to the water. After an hour or so,

something took my Sandy Mite and moved
slow and deep, deliberate, away—
a heavy throb like nothing I'd ever felt.
I waded around for maybe ten minutes
to get some line back, but the hook
pulled out. I never saw the fish.
In forty years it's gained a lot of weight.
We must have caught some other fish too,
but I don't remember them. That night
we traded beers at the long bar and trudged
upstairs to our room. At two a.m.
I woke to the moist smell of whiskey
and the rough touch of someone crawling
into my sheets. WHAT THE F***
ARE YOU DOING? I shouted to the dark.
A drunk had stumbled into our room
and taken off his clothes. I don't know
which of us was more surprised. He grabbed
his stuff and stuttered out to the hall.
I don't remember
anything else about that trip to Dillon.

Spawning Rainbows

I've lurked along the riverbanks
silly in the thistles
to watch fish sex from the willows.
Imagine doing it weightless:
circle, kick up gravel fighting bucks,
stop to watch the other's colors blaze
wildly more than functional,
begin slow rubbing. Escalate
till milt billows over fertile skeins
to sparkle all the eggs to full flower.
This genesis, this river birds and bees,
is miracle as great as galaxies.

Kinni Trip

I'd drive from the Twin Cities
After work to the Kinnickinnic,
The Willow or the Rush. The Kinni
Was my favorite, its tannic

Flows and hearty browns like tonic
For a weary trial lawyer caught
In the law's seamless web. My rod
And waders, vest and flies for trout

Were stashed with my lucky hat
In my trunk at all times just
In case a case got settled without
A trial or one of my clients confessed.

I'd usually head right for the best
Stretch at the end of a cul-de-sac
In a housing tract that went bust.
I'd park, gear up, and walk

Down the hill through maple and oak
And under a towering Linden tree
To the river where I had to look
Back like Orpheus to see

If my rusty old Eurydice
Up the hill was still there
Among the houses not to be
And the paved roads to nowhere.

Evening Hatch on the Willow

Sulphur duns drift down. Most
Are sipped by trout if they don't lift in flight.
Transparent spinners fly through thinning light
To dip their birth-wicks in the river host.
Emerging duns-to-be swim purposefully
Upward from the rocks. The sun exchanges
Places with the moon while wind arranges
Shadows on the water. Death's beauty
Magnifies unerring swoops of swallows.
Neither slurping trout nor flightborn hiss
Of bats deters the mating. They came for this.
I wade from the main current into the shallows.
My boots are bombs among the mayflies near
The bank. I am the only stranger here.

a kinnickinnic life

water opens—
a million still-wet wings
silent as flowers

waft in arabesques
marry in the flash
of bats and swallows

dip their eggs
till morning's fall—
water closes

The Encounter

Friday night, early September, rainy,
on my way from Bozeman to the Bighorn
I stopped in Livingston to call Gael.
He said not to bother. Five days
of rain had turned the Horn to pea green.
I turned south on Highway 89
to find a room for the night in Gardiner.
The one room left in town was pricey,
but Charlie Dog loved it (snuck him in).
We got up early and headed for Slough Creek,
breakfast and our lunch in the cooler.
It felt like the rain might turn to snow.
The two cars in line at the Park gate
later stopped in Mammoth. We owned the road.
There were no cars at any of the turnouts
when we got to Slough Creek. Unbelievable.
I suited up, let Charlie out to pee,
and hiked down the hill toward the creek.
In this lower stretch the fish get pounded
way more than in the serpentine
meanders of the meadows up above.
But up there it's all Yellowstone Cutts;
down here the bigger faster water
also holds some bruiser Rainbows.
Walking down I didn't see any rises.
I sat down to wait for the wind to drop
on the lee side of a boulder by the river,
my back against the rock, and scanned the brown
hills for elk or bison, maybe wolves.
The wind was strong enough to make that sound
wind makes when it whips around a rock
and cover any sound that I might make,

like boot scrapes, clearing of my throat
or rustling rain jacket. I barely heard
a tongue lapping water, as if Charlie
had left the car and come down to join me.
I slowly turned my head to the right
and there was a coyote, head down,
drinking about a rod length away,
completely unaware that I was there.
His eyes were yellowy grey, his left ear
slightly rumpled over
like an old war wound that never healed.
His lip was curled up like a dog's
to keep it out of the way while he drank.
I could see his tongue moving in and out,
his legs slightly splayed on the bank
so he could reach the water without
getting his paws wet. I couldn't see
his tail—only his front half stuck
out past the rock. Suddenly his head
snapped up and jerked toward me,
a smooth digital-quick move like
a bird's. He studied me for one beat
as if to make sure I was real,
then disappeared so
fast that except for the hairs
still standing up on my neck,
I wouldn't have believed it really happened.
And one thing I still can't decide:
was this an encounter with the other
or a brother?

Bighorn 1, You 0

The Horn is like a big spring creek
with flat flows faster than they look
and massive hatches: midges, baetis, caddis,
PMD's, tricos, and Yellow Sallies.
Wade around in PMD falls
picking off the sippers with a spinner
at Power Line, Crow Beach or Pipeline.
Try to find the bows among the browns—
they're bigger, faster, more spectacular.
See that silver head big as a beaver's
bobbing up and down greedily?
Better change your tippet, check your knots.
For the next half hour watch her feed
as the sun sets across her ripple patterns,
her head becoming dark in molten silver.
Your tiny fly matches the naturals
and so gets lost. You try a bigger fly.
There, now you can see it. So can she.
She comes a foot over to take it down,
her head blots it out, you set the hook.
You feel her bulk, she feels the hook and runs
across the river so fast you can't believe it,
faster than your reel with water spraying
up the line. Suddenly it all goes
limp. Your heart thumps so hard you hear
its bass line beneath your riff of groans.
You wade to the bank and sit down.
She was the biggest trout of your misspent life.
At first you're angry, playing it over and over.
Then the moon comes up on your favorite river,
its bright swath lighting up those seconds
burned into your brain like muscle memory,
transcendent as your first lost love.
You stand up and splash back to the boat
to tell your Bighorn buddies all about it.

Below the Bighorn Afterbay

Trucks back trailers, crunching gravel.
Over the lapping of drift boats in the water,
men and a few women shout directions,
point at distant clouds and realize
they didn't bring rain jackets.
They're threading fly line through the guides,
hanging cameras around their necks,
and coming out of the cement-block outhouse
pulling waders up. Boxes of flies
are opened on the spot, and eager fishers
wade out to cast as their buddies
trot down the hill from parking the truck.
The boats afloat are using indicators.
A mossy smell suffuses everything
as a guide and his sport in the stern
crack jokes. The guy in the bow is silent,
not even looking up to see the Pryors
or the river right rocks where the guide
squints the glare for signs of an emergence.
They slide past the Meat Hole
where five fishermen who walked down
have flailed for a good hour already,
each in his own world: cast, mend,
watch, pick it up, do it again.
A few flies appear, nothing taking
yet, but the guide studies them,
keeps up his patter for the sports,
and back-rows to keep the offerings
drifting just so. At the wing dam
where Ken Miyata was last seen in 1983
before his body was found, a camera
hanging from the neck and fly line
wrapped around him like a winding sheet,
some duns appear. Maybe by Second Island
the hogs will start to feed.

Ballad of a Bighorn Guide

for Ann

From 1982 to 2002
    for three hundred days a year,
Gael the guide was as common a sight
    on the Bighorn as heron or deer.

On October 17 of 2002
    at Three Mile he put in,
with old St. Pete in the bow seat
    and St. John in the stern.

These holy sports had heard reports
    of the best guide in the land.
They meant to catch the trico hatch,
    celestial rods in hand.

His oars were long, his arms were strong,
    he drank neither beer nor liquor.
He didn't smoke but liked a joke,
    on his gunwale a "No Whining" sticker.

I smile to tell he rowed like hell
    for Pipeline, but here's the rub:
had to make the hole, God save his soul,
    before the Rod and Gun Club.

Four miles to go when he started to row,
    the Club, four hundred yards.
But he knew those heads would stay in their beds
    to sleep off the booze and the cards.

He reached his first goal, the Snag Hole,
    then on to Duck Blind Channel.
(For fun he called it Tepee Run,
    for that was its Indian handle.)

He got himself to the S.B.A. Shelf,
    to Owl Tree and on to Crow Beach.
He rowed in style past old Six Mile
    till Bonefish Flats he reached.

He got to Pipeline in plenty of time
    so a message he could send:
He's already there in the pre-dawn air
    when the club members round the bend.

These worthies, hung over, at last come over,
    of their prowess they're so proud.
"Gentlemen!" says Gael, so goes the tale,
    and then he laughs out loud.

Their eyes are blinking, the members thinking
    Who are these ghosts in the fog?
"Good God" says one as he starts to run,
    "it's time for some hair of the dog."

In a voice so clear they still can hear
    Gael's words ring out in the cold:
"You'd be underway by yesterday
    to beat this guide to the hole."

Then he takes Peter's tippet—his fingers could grip it
    no matter how tiny the fly—
and ties that line with a knot so fine
    it's blind to the mortal eye.

He grabs the net, having won his bet,
    and giving St. Peter a wink,
says "We're on a roll, there's fish in this hole,
    Let's get 'em, what do you think?"

They say at night, if the wind's just right,
    dark moon and overcast,
you can hear Gael's boat out for a float
    and laughter as he rows past.

To the Bighorn Cabin, Burned

Our dream of you was drawn on a napkin.
We planned the slant of light through all your windows.
I hear re-membered walls bounce back the sounds
of Gael and Salvin pounding nails,
of cattle scratching backs on cottonwoods,
of laughter locked out naked in the hot tub,
of Charlie's barks, the pop of bacon grease,
the sibilance of fly rods pushed together,
the hoots of that little owl we took to the vet.
Eleven feet of cement were your foundation,
then ten-inch logs all linked ingeniously.
No river flood could have moved you,
but a hot wind blew sparks across the river,
and all that's left of you is these words.

Steelhead and Salmon

Tying a Steelhead Fly

Tying flies is mostly preparation
and ritual: fill favorite glass,
the one with the trout on the side,
with ice and a good single-malt.
Place glass on near right corner
of old roll-top desk you use to tie.
Sit down. Pick up glass
and take first sip. Smack lips.
Scratch chin and think about
what fly to tie—Steelhead Bee?
Don't feel like spinning all that hair.
How 'bout a nice Silver Hilton?
Sounds good. Start opening drawers
to look for black chenille, grizzly hackle,
a piece of oval silver tinsel ribbing,
and Mallard flank fibers for the tail.
Hmm, have to substitute for that one.
And where are all my new spey hooks?
Reach for glass, take another sip.
Fumble breast pocket. Oh, yeah,
I quit smoking. Turn on the light.
Open more drawers. Stand up
to stretch, sit down again. Reach
for glass and take another sip. Mmm.
Go to the refrigerator for ice
and more Scotch. Go to bathroom.
Walk back to desk and sit down.
Let's see now, where was I.

King of the Pier in Manitowoc

He's out before dawn in the fog
beside his pail of alewives on the pier
with lantern, roll of blankets, jelly doughnuts,
bottle of Four Roses, Sunday paper.
Between foghorn blasts which shape his shouts,
he steps into his casts with the long rod.
His shoulders coil and whirl, his hands
whip the rod like a violent wand. His cap,
a blue dot in all the grey, bobs
above his denim jacket, jeans so wet
they're almost black, and motorcycle boots.
The king is there more hours, his casts go
further out, he catches more King Salmon.
Still incomplete, he reaches over and over
for another silver lover.

Clearwater Reverie

The trees have just begun to turn,
The nights are cool and clear.
Your black and purple flies are ready.
You dream while drinking a beer:
Behind the rocks of Haystack Pool
Steelhead start to school.

You're casting with the long rod,
Whipping the snap-T
With snake rolls slick as a rope trick
Eighty feet effortlessly.
Let the wind blow with its fall might,
Your loops will still be tight.

These fish have come five hundred miles
Through eight big dams,
The Columbia, Snake, and Clearwater,
No maps or diagrams,
Nothing but Nature's cold fire
Burning with desire.

A cloudy day—it rained last night—
Your mind does the math:
Your fly will make a perfect wake,
Two eyes will watch its path.
A bulge as fish and fly are one,
Then that first run.

Your reel is like the squeaky wheel
That didn't get the grease.
With leader under stress you mentally
Call the knot police.
Your debts and failings sublimate
To a way higher state.

To a Wild Hen Steelhead

Up the Columbia, up the Snake,
Up the Clearwater, past eight dams,
Five hundred miles you swam
With your golden eggs to Haystack.

You've tasted fresh and salt water,
Outrun seals and killer whales
For years. What fabulous fishy tales
You could tell! And now I want to

Kiss you on your steely nose,
Return you to your air to find
Your way to the Selway, mind
Set on the place your mother chose

Four years ago, the cold
Gravel bed where ecstasy
And predators like bears and me
Will make you too soon old.

The Big One That . . .

for Frank L.

Every fall for ten years
I followed Lewis and Clark over Lolo Pass
along the Lochsa and the Clearwater
to Lewiston, Idaho to fish for steelhead.
I stayed at a cheap motel across the highway
from the Stink Hole where a pulp mill
belched day and night. I didn't care.
I'd start there every morning and work my way
up through Truck, Cat, Coyote Fishnet,
Ant and Yellowjacket, Park, and Haystack.

On October 11, 1996,
below Haystack island my Green Butt Skunk
was swinging across the current when it
stopped, then moved away slowly.
I should get out and follow this one down,
but it was too deep to cross to either bank.
That fish was on for more than twenty minutes—
three long unhurried runs, no jumps,
and after each run I'd work him all the way
back to the riffle where I could see him
clearly in the high sun: the dark back
and long red stripes over silver,
but I couldn't budge his bulk any closer.

At last I got impatient, clamped down
and backed up the rocks. His big head
coming in toward me managed one more
shake. My frayed leader
popped. He floundered there for a moment—
I dropped my rod and stumbled into the water.
He slipped away. I fell
down on my knees, hands out.
Two guys who watched the whole thing
from the far bank both shook their heads
and went back to casting.

First Coast Steelhead

Years of zeroes, the Oregon horse collar,
ended one gray day in rain forest
on the gravel bar of a small coastal stream,
vines and dripping ferns on both banks.
My planets were aligned, trajectories
of fish and fly intersected
and BINGO, even the willows wept for joy.
But synapses short-circuited and zap—
aurora borealis of the brain.
My fat fingers couldn't reel the reel
and line was peeling out like a Koufax fastball.
Even in the shallows I could barely see her:
her body was a mirror in the water.
At last on my knees I reached out
to touch her gravid flank of minted coin,
ore from heaven's mine, silver ingot.
Her eyes were distillations of farthest stars.
I kissed her on the nose: water mother,
go make more.

Salmon Love

Here's to Pacific Salmon
Who run in fall to mate
With singular purpose. Examine
Why they come so late

In life, for such an act
Of lust requires strength
To reach the place their pact
With sex is sealed. A length

Of river home traversed,
The siren song of falls
Jumped to woo and burst
With procreation. She calls

Him to her water bed
And flirts with silver thigh.
For love they'll soon be dead,
But what a way to die.

To a Dead King Salmon

Handsome one, you could have graced a table
or made the day of an old fisherman
by taking his homemade fly and coming to hand.

Instead your iridescence putrifies
to ride indifferent currents downstream
and bounce along the bottom of deep holes.

Perhaps an eagle will find you and be sated,
his hooked beak tearing out your eyes
and ripping through your skin to pick your liver.

Or cast out of your element altogether,
you'll wash up on a bar to squabbling gulls
while hungry crayfish click insistent claws.

You gave your life to mate with a hen
and gave your milky blessing to her redd.
Your love was true and won't be given again.

What sort of life swam in your submarine,
your scaly ship with gills and caudal fin?
And where did it go, now that it can fly?

The Salt

Battle on Florida Bay, 1976

The shallow flats are empty
except for the tarpon. He hangs
above the sea grass, moored to his shadow.
His undershot jaw juts
from scales the size of dinner plates.
I cast my fly in front of his face,
let it sit. Twitch it. The iron lips
open slowly, close with a soundless clang.
I set the hook hard twice and he
shatters the water, glistens in the shards
like a silver missile. Then for an hour
he's a train on a water prairie
making time between water cities
and I'm just hanging on.
Two hours. The fish still
shoulders through the waves.
My lips are welts in the sun.
My shoulders pull out with the line.
The heat squeezes visions taut:
run the fish-flag up,
hang his bulk at the dock,
tourists take his picture, poke his flanks.
Three hours. His prehistoric armor
rattles in a last jump. Will the tired sea-engine
hiss to a stop, all battles won but this?
Will he fish-scream when I lift him into air
to preserve in remembrance of me?
Near the boat his starboard eye
looks at me. I cannot do it.
I cut the line. We both are free.

Magnificent Frigate-Bird

She glides near
the open sea
without fear
ceaselessly.

Her pterodactyl
wing feather
lacks the oil
to repel water.

If she should fall
from blue to blue
the sea's her pall
and bearer too.

In Mexico After Too Much Rum I Obsess About Tomorrow's Fishing

I.

In January off the Yucatan
I listen in my bed at Playa Blanca
To the sea settle down the Sian Ka'an.

Manana chachalacas' raucous cackles
Will talk to me of coffee strong and black
And high clean sun will warm the flats.

My dreams fill up with Palometas grandes
Rooting in the sand, their black tails
Slipping like a sickle through the surface.

They mingle with a school of mudding bones
While tarpon tow their long silver banners
Through all the undulating blues and greens.

II.

In January off the Yucatan
I listen in my bed at Playa Blanca
To breakers bash the beach at Sian Ka'an.

Manana chachalaca caca piles
My room as vultures circle skies so vile
The sun decides to go back down for a while.

My nightmare is a sloppy cast that sails
High into the mangroves till a gale
Whips it into knots the size of bales

Which sink the hook into my testicle
And tie me up in a big gnarly ball
To thrash away in fluorocarbon hell.

GT Quickstep

The search for bones
        on Christmas Island's endless flats—
your eyes sweep side
        to side across the sand and darker marl
and pick through the undulating weeds—
        is suddenly interrupted when the
blue metallic glint, the fleeting
        almost-shape of a Giant Trevally
maybe two or three GT's
        appear and ripple erratically
across your line of sight.
        You yell for the guide who's got
your ten-weight with the big crab fly
        and start thrashing toward him through
heavy salt water
        while reeling in your bonefish fly and
hooking it to the rod, arm outstretched
        to hand the lighter outfit off
grab the GT stick and strip
        line out as you thrash back through
heavy salt water
        and try to get as close as you . . .
where the heck are they?
        There they are, pretty far out
maybe you can still do it
        whip the rod back and forth
strip out more, more, more . . .
        Shit.

The Answer

Various blues—turquoise,
Purple, lavender—
In rolling equipoise
Are Ocean's lavish answer

To every question.
In deeps and far reefs
Ocean floods her children
With blue beliefs:

Life is a blue dream.
You are a blue song.
Death is a blue dream.
Ocean is never wrong.

Last Casts

fish mystics

fish are of the water
more than we are of the earth
for we do not breathe the earth
nor does earth enfold us while we live
and fish are of the water more
than birds are of the air
for even when fish die
gravity does not overcome them
the element they used to breathe
that held them all their life
still holds them when they are no more
until they are more
water

Yellowstone Pictures

Juniper perfume
in a meadow lush with lupine
glosses over the slump of talus
and sagebrush's turn to tumbleweed.

Tourist tennis shoes
toe painted rocks
that still bear the prints of moccasins.

At the Buffalo Bill Museum
the Chief Joseph statue
keeps turning away from the camera.

At Nez Perce Creek
I take a snapshot
of Bobby with buffalo,
his twelve-year-old smile in full sun.

A Lone Fisherman Not Alone

Out along the Redwood Highway, half way from Grants Pass to the coast, I was sneaking looks at the Middle Fork of the Smith and almost passed the campground across from the Patrick Creek Inn where the Stump Hole is. Steelheading legends like Bill Schaadt and Russell Chatham used to fish this hole and later wrote about it. California back then, to put it mildly, had better steelhead runs. You didn't have to drive this far from San Francisco to have a good time on the Russian or the Eel to name two.

I stopped to have a look. There was an old Datsun with Illinois plates, mustard colored and rusty around the edges, parked far back under the trees. I walked in without even suiting up or bringing a rod. I didn't have the time and besides, it was another miserable year, the steelhead run practically non-existent. Even with bait, which unbelievably was still allowed, nobody was catching anything.

There's no stump in the Stump Hole now, but it's still got the classic look: current along the far bank, slower water closer in, a long run where you can step, cast, step for more than an hour, then walk upstream and do it again. A guy was fishing the hole, his two-handed rod swinging slowly, almost casting itself, with snake rolls rolling over and over all the way across the river.

As the lone fisherman turned to walk back upstream, I saw that he was young, twenty-five at most, with black hair under an old Forty-Niners ball cap, a worn wool shirt, and rubber waders held up by makeshift suspenders pinned together with safety pins. The reel on his bamboo rod was nicked and black like a big Pflueger Medalist.

"Any luck?" I asked him when he got close enough, knowing what the answer would be.

"Yes, sir," he grinned as he sat down on a rock, "but not with the fish."

"Well, what other kind of luck is there?" was my smart reply.

He laughed. "For the last three years I've fished this hole every day for a week in January. Never caught a thing. It doesn't matter. This was my dad's rod and reel, these were his waders, this was his hat. He taught me everything: how to cast, how to tie flies, how to wade. This was his favorite hole in his favorite river at this time of year. I live in Chicago now, but I drive out every January and fish this hole just like he did, even sit on the same damn rock. It's more like a dance than real fishing, so I always have good luck."

Lake Michigan Vespers

The pier slips through, and through
The grasp of slate-grey fingers.
Father Dark kneels on the clouds
Where a blush of daylight lingers.

Gulls like crosses in the wind
Cry down the sounding sun
As genuflecting fishing boats
Chant on their homeward run.

Foghorns, organs of the night,
Their bass vibratos play.
Mother Eve lights votive stars
To mourn the death of day.

The Eagle

He watched us from his tree.
Inside the car
my son pointed him out to me.
We were free
to pass as if he weren't there,

but he was. I stopped the car
to study him.
He looked old and far
from home where
nobody stared at him.

Resigned as if that limb
were his last,
all the rest of them
over time's rim,
his future and his past

gathered there to rest
in a present
that now included us, his last
witnesses, who lost
all except this final element.

Do Not Go Gentle

When I am too old,
Mary will strap a fly rod to my wrist
and push me in a wheelchair to the end
of the pier where I can
half-cast and drool into my vest
until a surf perch tugs my indicator
under, waking synapses
that set me madly reeling till I
reel in the sea.

About the Author

Harry Piper is a retired trial attorney and ranch real estate agent who lives with his wife Mary, an Episcopal priest and breast cancer survivor, and two of their children, Andy and Risa, on the banks of the Rogue River near Medford, Oregon. (Their son Bob lives with his wife Molly and their three children in the Seattle area.) He has been a fisherman for almost 60 years, and a fly fisherman most of that time. He is past president of the Whirling Disease Foundation, a lifetime member of Trout Unlimited, and a member of the Federation of Fly Fishers, Rogue Fly Fishers, Steamboaters, the Native Fish Society, and The Freshwater Trust (formerly Oregon Trout). His fishing articles and poetry have appeared or been accepted for publication in *Fly Fisherman, Gray's Sporting Journal, Jefferson Monthly, Minnesota Monthly, Twin Cities*, and other publications. This is his first book.